MW00892759

THIS IS A COFFEE TABLE BOOK

Copyright © 2023

All rights reserved.

No part of this publication may be reproduced, distributed, or transmitted in any form or by any means, including photocopying, recording, or other electronic or mechanical methods, without the prior written permission of the publisher, except in the case of brief quotations embodied in critical reviews and certain other noncommercial uses permitted by copyright law.

COFFEE TABLE ART

[Agency FB]

COFFEE

TABLE ART

[ALGERIAN]

COFFEE TABLE ART

[AR BERKLEY]

COFFEE TABLE ART

[AR Blanca]

COFFEE TABLE ART

[AR BONNIE]

COFFEE

TABLE ART

[AR CARTER]

COFFEE
TABLE ART

[AR CENA]

COFFEE
TABLE ART

[AR CHRISTY]

COFFEE

TABLE ART

[AR DARLING]

COFFEE TABLE

ART

[AR DECODE]

COFFEE
TABLE ART

[AR DELANEY]

COFFEE TABLE

ART

[AR DESTINE]

COFFEE TABLE

ART

[AR ESSENCE]

COFFEE TABLE ART

ART

[AR HERMANN]

COFFEE
TABLE ART

[AR JULIAN]

COFFEE TABLE ART

[Arial]

COFFEE
TABLE ART

[Arial Black]

COFFEE TABLE ART

[Arial Narrow]

COFFEE
TABLE ART

[Arial Rounded MT Bold]

COFFEE TABLE ART

[AvenirLT-Medium]

COFFEE TABLE ART

[AvenirLT-Roman]

COFFEE TABLE ART

[Bahnschrift]

COFFEE TABLE ART

[Bahnschrift Condensed]

COFFEE
TABLE ART

[Bahnschrift Light]

COFFEE TABLE ART

[Bahnschrift Light Condensed]

COFFEE TABLE
ART

[Bahnschrift Light SemiCondensed]

COFFEE
TABLE ART

[Bahnschrift Light SemiBold]

COFFEE TABLE ART

[Bahnschrift Light SemiBold Condensed]

COFFEE TABLE ART

[Bahnschrift Light SemiBold SemiCondensed]

COFFEE TABLE ART

[Bahnschrift SemiCondensed]

COFFEE
TABLE ART

[Bahnschrift SemiLight]

COFFEE TABLE ART

[Bahnschrift SemiLight Condensed]

COFFEE TABLE

ART

[Bahnschrift SemiLight SemiCondensed]

COFFEE
TABLE
ART

[Basekerville Old Face]

COFFEE TABLE ART

[Bahaus 93]

COFFEE TABLE ART

[Bell MT]

COFFEE TABLE ART

ART

[Berlin Sans FB]

COFFEE TABLE ART

[Berlin Sans FB Demi]

COFFEE TABLE

ART

[Bernard MT Condensed]

COFFEE

TABLE

ART

[Blackadder ITC]

COFFEE TABLE ART

[Bodoni MT]

COFFEE TABLE

ART

[Bodoni MT Black]

COFFEE TABLE ART

[Bodoni MT Condensed]

COFFEE TABLE ART

[Bodoni MT Poster Condensed]

COFFEE TABLE ART

[Book Antiqua]

COFFEE
TABLE ART

[Bookman Old Style]

COFFEE TABLE ART

[Bradley Hand ITC]

COFFEE TABLE ART

[Britannic Bold]

COFFEE TABLE ART

[Broadway]

COFFEE TABLE ART

[Brush Script MT]

COFFEE TABLE ART

[Calibri]

COFFEE TABLE

ART

[Calibri Light]

COFFEE TABLE

ART

[Californian FB]

COFFEE TABLE

ART

[Calisto MT]

COFFEE
TABLE ART

[Cambria]

COFFEE
TABLE ART

[Cambria Math]

COFFEE TABLE ART

[Candara]

COFFEE TABLE ART

[Candara Light]

COFFEE TABLE ART

[CASTELLAR]

COFFEE TABLE ART

[Centaur]

COFFEE
TABLE ART

[Century]

COFFEE TABLE ART

[Century Gothic]

COFFEE
TABLE ART

[Century Schoolbook]

COFFEE TABLE

ART

[Chiller]

COFFEE TABLE ART

ART

[Colonna MT]

COFFEE
TABLE ART

[Comic Sans MS]

COFFEE
TABLE ART

⌊Consolas⌋

COFFEE TABLE ART

[Constantia]

COFFEE TABLE ART

[Cooper Black]

COFFEE TABLE ART

[Copperplate Gothic Bold]

COFFEE TABLE

ART

[Copperplate Gothic Light]

COFFEE
TABLE ART

[Corbel]

149

COFFEE
TABLE ART

[Corbel Light]

COFFEE
TABLE ART

[Courier New]

COFFEE TABLE

ART

[Curlz MT]

COFFEE TABLE ART

[Ebrima]

COFFEE TABLE ART

ART

[Edwardian Script ITC]

COFFEE
TABLE ART

[ELEPHANT]

COFFEE TABLE ART

[ENGRAVERS MT]

COFFEE TABLE ART

[Eras Bold ITC]

COFFEE
TABLE ART

[Eras Demi ITC]

COFFEE
TABLE ART

[Eras Light ITC]

COFFEE TABLE ART

[Eras Medium ITC]

COFFEE
TABLE ART

[FELIX TITLING]

173

COFFEE TABLE ART

[Fontdinerdotcom Sparkly]

COFFEE TABLE
ART

[Footlight MT Light]

COFFEE TABLE ART

[Forte]

COFFEE TABLE ART

[Franklin Gothic Book]

COFFEE TABLE ART

[Franklin Gothic Demi]

COFFEE
TABLE ART

[Franklin Gothic Demi Cond]

COFFEE TABLE ART

[Franklin Gothic Heavy]

COFFEE TABLE ART

[Franklin Gothic Medium]

COFFEE TABLE ART

[Franklin Gothic Medium Cond]

COFFEE TABLE ART

[Freestyle Script]

COFFEE TABLE ART

[French Script MT]

COFFEE TABLE

ART

[Gabriola]

COFFEE
TABLE ART

[Gadugi]

COFFEE TABLE ART

[Garamond]

COFFEE
TABLE ART

[Georgia]

COFFEE TABLE ART

[Gigi]

COFFEE TABLE

ART

[Gill Sans MT]

COFFEE TABLE ART

ART

[Gill Sans MT Condensed]

COFFEE TABLE

ART

[Gill Sans MT Ext Condensed Bold]

COFFEE TABLE ART

[Gill Sans Ultra Bold]

COFFEE TABLE ART

[Gill Sans Ultra Bold Condensed]

COFFEE TABLE ART

[Gloucester MT Extra Condensed]

COFFEE TABLE
ART

[Goudy Old Style]

COFFEE
TABLE ART

[Goudy Stout]

COFFEE TABLE ART

[Haettenschweiler]

COFFEE TABLE ART

[Harlow Solid Italic]

COFFEE TABLE
ART

[Harrington]

COFFEE TABLE ART

[High Tower Text]

COFFEE TABLE

ART

[HoloLens MDL2 Assets]

COFFEE TABLE

ART

[Impact]

COFFEE
TABLE ART

[Imprint MT Shadow]

COFFEE TABLE

ART

[Informal Roman]

COFFEE
TABLE ART

[Ink Free]

COFFEE

TABLE ART

[Javanese Text]

COFFEE TABLE ART

[Jokerman]

COFFEE TABLE ART

[Juice ITC]

COFFEE TABLE ART

[Kristen ITC]

COFFEE TABLE ART

[Kunstler Script]

COFFEE
TABLE ART

[Leelawadee]

COFFEE
TABLE ART

[Leelawadee UI]

COFFEE TABLE ART

[Leelawadee UI Semilight]

COFFEE TABLE ART

[Lucida Bright]

COFFEE TABLE ART

[Lucida Calligraphy]

COFFEE TABLE
ART

[Lucida Console]

COFFEE
TABLE ART

[Lucida Fax]

COFFEE TABLE

ART

[Lucida Handwriting]

COFFEE TABLE ART

[Lucida Sans]

COFFEE TABLE ART

[Lucida Sans Typewriter]

COFFEE
TABLE ART

[Lucida Sans Unicode]

COFFEE TABLE ART

[Magneto]

COFFEE TABLE ART

[Maiandra GD]

COFFEE

TABLE ART

[Malgun Gothic]

COFFEE TABLE

ART

[Malgun Gothic Semilight]

COFFEE TABLE ART

[Matura MT Script Capitals]

COFFEE TABLE ART

[Microsoft Himalaya]

COFFEE

TABLE ART

[Microsoft JhengHei]

COFFEE

TABLE ART

[Microsoft JhengHei Light]

COFFEE
TABLE ART

[Microsoft JhengHei UI]

COFFEE

TABLE ART

[Microsoft JhengHei UI Light]

COFFEE TABLE ART

[Microsoft New Tai Lue]

COFFEE TABLE ART

[Microsoft PhagsPa]

COFFEE TABLE ART

[Microsoft Sans Serif]

COFFEE
TABLE ART

[Microsoft Tae Le]

COFFEE TABLE

ART

[Microsoft Uighur]

COFFEE

TABLE ART

[Microsoft YaHei]

COFFEE
TABLE ART

[Microsoft YaHei Light]

COFFEE

TABLE ART

[Microsoft YaHei UI]

COFFEE

TABLE ART

[Microsoft YaHei UI Light]

COFFEE TABLE ART

[Microsoft Yi Baiti]

COFFEE TABLE
ART

[MingLiU_HKSCS-ExtB]

COFFEE TABLE ART

ART

[MingLiU-ExtB]

COFFEE

TABLE ART

[Mistral]

COFFEE
TABLE ART

[Modern No. 20]

COFFEE
TABLE ART

[Mongolian Baiti]

COFFEE TABLE

ART

[Monotype Corsiva]

COFFEE TABLE ART

[MS Gothic]

COFFEE
TABLE ART

[MS PGothic]

COFFEE TABLE ART

[MS Reference Sans Serif]

COFFEE
TABLE ART

[MS UI Gothic]

COFFEE

TABLE ART

[MV Boli]

COFFEE

TABLE ART

[Myanmar Text]

COFFEE TABLE ART

[Niagara Engraved]

COFFEE TABLE ART

[Niagara Solid]

COFFEE

TABLE ART

[Nirmala UI]

COFFEE TABLE ART

ART

[Nirmala UI Semilight]

COFFEE TABLE
ART

[NSimSum]

COFFEE
TABLE ART

【OCR A Extended】

COFFEE TABLE ART

[OCR B MT]

COFFEE TABLE ART

[OCR-A II]

COFFEE TABLE ART

[Old English Text MT]

COFFEE TABLE ART

[Onyx]

COFFEE TABLE ART

[Palace Script MT]

COFFEE
TABLE ART

[Palatino Linotype]

COFFEE TABLE ART

[Papyrus]

[Parchment]

COFFEE
TABLE
ART

[Perpetua]

COFFEE TABLE ART

[Perpetua Titling mt]

COFFEE TABLE

ART

[Playbill]

COFFEE
TABLE ART

[PMingLiU-ExtB]

COFFEE TABLE ART

[Poor Richard]

COFFEE TABLE ART

[Pristina]

COFFEE TABLE ART

[QuickType II]

COFFEE TABLE ART

[QuickType II Condensed]

COFFEE TABLE ART

[QuickType II Mono]

COFFEE TABLE
ART

[Quick Type IIPi]

COFFEE TABLE ART

(Rage Italic)

COFFEE TABLE

ART

[Ravie]

COFFEE
TABLE ART

[Rockwell]

COFFEE
TABLE ART

[Rockwell Condensed]

COFFEE
TABLE ART

[Rockwell Extra Bold]

COFFEE TABLE ART

[Script MT Bold]

COFFEE TABLE ART

[Segoe MDL2 Assets]

COFFEE TABLE ART

[Segoe Print]

COFFEE TABLE ART

ART

[Segoe Script]

COFFEE TABLE ART

[Segoe UI]

COFFEE TABLE ART

[Segoe UI Black]

COFFEE TABLE ART

[Segoe UI Emoji]

COFFEE TABLE ART

[Segoe UI Historic]

COFFEE TABLE ART

[Segoe UI Light]

COFFEE TABLE ART

[Segoe UI SemiBold]

COFFEE TABLE ART

[Segoe UI SemiLight]

COFFEE TABLE ART

[Segoe UI Symbol]

COFFEE TABLE ART

ART

[Showcard Gothic]

COFFEE TABLE ART

[SimSun]

COFFEE TABLE

ART

[SimSun-ExtB]

COFFEE TABLE ART

[Sitka Banner]

COFFEE TABLE ART

[Sitka Display]

COFFEE TABLE ART

[Sitka Heading]

COFFEE TABLE ART

[Sitka Small]

COFFEE TABLE ART

[Sitka Subheading]

COFFEE
TABLE ART

[Sitka Text]

COFFEE TABLE ART

[Snap ITC]

COFFEE TABLE ART

[STENCIL]

COFFEE TABLE ART

[Sylfaen]

ΦΥΧΚ

[Σψμβολ]

COFFEE
TABLE ART

[Tahoma]

COFFEE TABLE

ART

[Tempus Sans ITC]

COFFEE
TABLE ART

[Times New Roman]

COFFEE
TABLE ART

[Trebuchet MS]

COFFEE TABLE ART

[Tw Cen MT]

COFFEE TABLE

ART

[Tw Cen MT Condensed]

COFFEE TABLE

ART

[Tw Cen MT Condensed Extra Bold]

COFFEE
TABLE ART

[Verdana]

COFFEE TABLE ART

[Viner Hand ITC]

COFFEE TABLE ART

[Vivaldi]

COFFEE TABLE ART

[Vladimir Script]

COFF EE TABL E ART

[Wide Latin]

COFFEE

TABLE ART

[Yu Gothic]

COFFEE

TABLE ART

[Yu Gothic Light]

COFFEE
TABLE ART

[Yu Gothic Medium]

COFFEE

TABLE ART

[Yu Gothic UI]

COFFEE TABLE

ART

[Yu Gothic UI Light]

COFFEE

TABLE ART

[Yu Gothic UI SemiBold]

COFFEE TABLE

ART

[Yu Gothic UI SemiLight]

COFFEE

TABLE ART

[Yu Mincho]

Made in the USA
Coppell, TX
12 October 2024

38559707R00267